A HOME IN

WALKER VALLEY

THE STORY OF TREMONT

BY JEREMY LLOYD

Contents

INTRODUCTION

This is the story of one place on earth, one river valley among many others in the Great Smoky Mountains. It was once known by names that are no longer used, such as Fodderstack Cove. Others like Walker Valley and Tremont have stuck. One descends into it, coming from the south at least, by way of the breakneck flanks of Devils Courthouse and Thunderhead Mountain. Tributaries bearing names such as Deerhobble, Lost Branch, and Stillhouse Hollow far below give birth to the Middle Prong of the Little River. The heartblood of the valley, the Middle Prong tumbles toward the Gulf of Mexico carrying away the mountains bit by bit as it has done for millennia.

The most easily accessible and, for many years, overlooked entrance to the valley resides near the Townsend Wye. Four decades after the first European-Americans began populating nearby Cades Cove, Walker Valley remained a virtually unknown wilderness. Long before that, the Cherokee crossed over the mountains via Indian Gap to the east and Spence Field to the west, yet forged no significant paths this way. Nevertheless, although there is scant evidence that Native Americans ever lived here, it's certain that they hunted game and harvested wild plants in these rich forests as long as ten thousand years ago.

Today a paved road welcomes visitors to Great Smoky Mountains Institute at Tremont, on acreage once farmed by Will and Nancy Walker. An auto tour of the logging era beckons further exploration along a gravel road that dead-ends deeper in the valley at the spot where a logging town once stood. The valley has seen a great many changes over the years. People who have called it home at one time or another each viewed the land in uniquely different ways according to their individual needs, their values, and the times they lived in. Joy and sorrow filled their lives in equal measure. A few lessons perhaps might be learned from them, and from events that once took place here. It is a story that in many ways echoes the bigger story of the Great Smokies, and the even bigger story of how humans view nature and interact with their environment.

Here, then, is the story of Tremont.

Big Will Walker

On Old Fodder Stack we hunted
All around Old Fodder Stack,
How we love them little green valleys,
And some day we are going back.

From "Smokey Mountain Song and Story Book"
by Leonard Marshal McCarter

WILL AND NANCY WALKER MUST HAVE THOUGHT THEY'D FOUND A PIECE OF heaven when they first stepped into the valley that would become their home for the rest of their lives. Giant Carolina silverbells and American chestnuts towered overhead. Deep shadows cast by the surrounding ridges further shaded the forest where the occasional wolf and mountain lion still roamed. Around them, phoebes and warblers and other forest denizens chattered to one another about the newcomers' arrival. And the river, always the sound of the river filled their ears.

Flat tillable bottomland was scarce in the valley, though just enough existed to meet their needs. Growing up in Rudd Hollow in Tuckaleechee Cove, Will had watched rain showers fall many times around a distant mountain shaped like a stack of winter livestock fodder. "I'm going to live at the foot of that mountain some day," he said during a particularly dry year when the corn in his parents' fields was withering.

Will and Nancy Walker arrived as newlyweds in the tiny cove nestled in the shadow of Fodderstack Mountain in 1859. Both of Scottish descent, they

Big Will Walker and his rifle, Ol' Death.

Ol' Death

Will Walker's father was a blacksmith by trade, and it was likely from him that he learned skills that enabled him to make his own hunting rifle. It would become famous in its day. Six feet in length, it was called Ol' Death for its accuracy at two hundred yards. Will constructed the stock out of wood he cut on his land in Walker Valley. Far more modern guns were common during his lifetime, but he preferred his muzzleloader to newfangled inventions. Famed writer Horace Kephart met the legendary hunter of Walker Valley once and learned a trick or two. Will told him that his two-ounce bullets were small enough to slip down the barrel by their own weight without the help of a ramrod, which was especially handy when he was in a hurry and had to get a shot off quick.

He'd pour in the powder, guessing the amount, wet the bullet in his mouth, and drop it down the barrel. Enough powder usually stuck to the ball to keep it from rolling out.

Will was full of hunting stories. One time there was a bear that eluded a group of hunters and escaped into a cave. The group's leader offered a cash prize to whomever would kill the bear. Will volunteered, entering the cave cautiously and moving forward step by step, his gun poised, until he felt the bear's warm, moist breath on his face. Firing

were 21 and 19 years old respectively. The oldest of fourteen children, William Marion was born the same year the Cherokee were marched westward on the Trail of Tears, 1838. His father was a circuit riding Covenant Presbyterian preacher and his mother belonged to the McGill clan of Scotland. He was a double first cousin to John Walker, father of the famous Walker sisters. Nancy Louisa's people were Caylors.

Like any young couple they were seeking a place to call their own. Three separate land grants totaling 5,200 acres enabled Will to acquire land extending from the Forks of the River (now the Townsend Wye) all the way to Thunderhead Prong. Throughout his life he traded and bought land, increasing the size of his kingdom.

The pair's first journey into the valley likely came by way of the Spicewoods via Schoolhouse Gap and the West Prong of the Little River. They carried seeds of plants with them for a garden and fruit orchards. They brought tools for use in building a house, including a broadax to hew round logs into square lumber; an adze to smooth it; and a froe and wooden club for splitting shingles made out of white oak. Chickens and a milking cow were likewise essential in order to start a farm. Skills, though, were perhaps their greatest asset, for without them they could not have survived in the wilderness. At times, gumption alone could be depended on. If high water prevented a trip to the hardware store in Tuckaleechee Cove, they lived by the motto, "Use it up, wear it out; make do or do without."

Running a farm meant dividing labors between husband and wife. Nancy spent long hours cooking over an open fire and tending a vegetable garden. She spun yarn, wove cloth and made all the clothes. Before long she was doing all that plus bearing children.

Numerous other labors fell on the shoulders of "Big" Will. Standing over six feet tall, he liked to refer to a giant tuliptree growing on his property as his "walking stick." He also came to be known as "Black" Will or "Black Bill," a moniker which helped to distinguish him from a redhead with the same name, though some genealogists claim the name belongs to a cousin and is therefore incorrectly applied.

He fashioned barrels and buckets out of tight-grained white oak wood. He husbanded peach and apple trees in his orchard which supplied fruit that was sliced and dried and kept as winter food. He pastured cattle and hogs which roamed freely yet were "salted" in order to keep them from becoming wild. He butchered hogs in fall when they were good and fat. After the meat was salted, it was placed in a "bran" sack made of cotton and hung in a smokehouse. Once it was cured it was stacked in a corner where slices could be drawn off for months and fed into a kettle.

A farm sled was Will's primary means for hauling. Later he purchased a factory-made wagon which had to be carried into the valley before it could be assembled since the path wasn't wide enough for it. His dependable red

Big Will Walker was the definition of resourceful. He could make anything, from a grist mill to a hunting rifle.

blindly, he managed to kill the bear in one shot and triumphantly exited the cave with his prize. He refused the money, however, knowing the bear's hide alone was worth far more than that. His marksmanship was so renowned that he was prohibited from competing in sharp-shooting contests. With Ol' Death he killed over a hundred bears in his lifetime.

Big Will Walker and his wife Nancy.

ox Ol' Berry was indispensable in pulling the limited amount of timber he sold.

Making his own millstones with a hammer and chisel, Will built three water-powered grist mills on his property. Wheat did not grow well in the valley, so corn became the main crop. Cornbread might be eaten three times a day. A typical supper might also have included bacon, beans, sweet potatoes and honey. The river provided a ready supply of trout, and the woods a cornucopia of turkeys, deer, squirrels, grouse, bears and raccoons to hunt.

Will kept more than a hundred beehives near his home and more still several miles deeper into the valley. He made each one out of hollow black gum logs which typically rot from the inside out. Will was a "bee-charmer." He didn't use smoke or a mask to rob honey from his bees, but instead would spray a mixture of honey and water from his mouth straight up into the air and let it fall on his head and shoulders. Rather than stinging him, bees would feed off the honey-water as he robbed their hive. He harvested honey twice a year: in spring when tuliptrees were in bloom, and in summer when sourwood trees flowered. In Tuckaleechee Cove a ten-pound can of honey fetched eighty cents to a dollar. He sold tons of honey over the years, often carrying it to market by hand.

Circumstances required Will to be a jack-of-all-trades. While outsiders might have considered him "uneducated," anyone whose education was limited to school and book-learning would have been ill-equipped in both mind and spirit to face the daunting challenges that life in the wilderness posed. Only a native intelligence such as his could have helped him accomplish the feat not merely of surviving but thriving in such an isolated setting.

Will took to heart what the Bible said about subduing and populating the earth. But to him subduing didn't mean taming something he loved. Instead,

Mary Ann Moore (center, front) was the second woman to join the Walker household.
Here she is with several of her children.

the freedom he possessed as a mountaineer meant conserving and preserving the wilderness. The wild, vast forest stood within 200 feet of the house and he liked it that way.

The Civil War broke out only a few years after Will and Nancy settled in the valley. In nearby Cades Cove many young men left home to fight for the Union while others sided with the Confederacy. Will never fought in the war himself. War got in the way of the liberty he'd found in the mountains. Though he never took sides, he joined his neighbors in Tuckaleechee Cove in helping to form a Home Guard against Confederate raiders who plundered remote and vulnerable mountain valleys. A relative of his joked that the reason he never fought in the war was so he could stay home and chase after women. Whatever his motives, Will did cut firewood for many women whose husbands were fighting and who otherwise might have frozen to death.

Ashley Moore

Ashley Moore was Will and Nancy's grandson through Loon Grant Moore and his first wife Betty Walker. Crippled in boyhood when a schoolmate threw a rock that struck his left leg, he spent most of his youth in pain. It didn't stop him though from mastering backwoods skills such as hunting and trapping, or from leading outsiders on fishing trips. Not until around age thirty did he receive medical treatment. The "treatment" was amputation of his leg. However, he was still an excellent swimmer, and aided by crutches he kept bees and continued running traplines for mink, muskrat, and raccoon. "He could go through these woods a whole lot faster than me," said Arnold Thompson who learned how to hunt 'coons from him. He inherited Ol' Death after Will died and continued the tradition of firing it at midnight on Christmas Eve. His main sources of income from selling honey and hides were intermittent, and he often struggled to get by. Hard up for cash, he sold Ol' Death. He also took up moonshining. Because his one leg would not make for a fast getaway should government revenuers close in, he was assigned the role of furnishing the supplies, buying the copper parts for the still and sugar and cornmeal for the mash. He knew his wife Myrtie, whom he called

The Family Grows

Will and Nancy read Scripture regularly noting that God had blessed and granted prosperity to David and other biblical patriarchs who took more than one wife. So following the war, when Will Walker met Mary Ann Moore in neighboring Sevier County (where she was serving as a midwife), he persuaded her to accompany him home. The fact that not as many men of marrying age were alive after the war as before may have factored into her decision.

The arrangement, though unconventional, was more than amicable between Nancy and Mary Ann. Indeed, it was Nancy's decision as much as it was Will's. Her last three children had all died in infancy, and soon she would be past her childbearing years altogether.

Ashley Moore and Sherman Watson.

*Moll Stinnett was the third of Will's three "wives."
She is shown here with six of her children, all dressed
up but with no shoes on, ca. 1910.*

There remained much work to do on the farm, and both she and Will wondered who would take care of them in old age. Will built Mary Ann a log cabin and deeded her several acres of land. They had eight children together. Nancy served as midwife for many of Mary Ann's children. Five would go on to attend Maryville College.

After several more years, when once again there were no more children at home, Will took a third wife, Mary "Moll" Stinnett, who happened to be younger than his oldest child. He built a cabin for her as well. Moll and Will

Sweetheart all his life, would never agree that they were so in need as to justify such a risk, so he kept his activities secret from her. Whenever she asked where he'd been, he'd say, "Sweetheart, I've been a-groundhog huntin'." One day he lingered at the still too long. The revenuers raided and Ashley went to jail. Myrtie refused to visit him, though she sent him every spare bit of money she acquired from honey sales so he could buy smoking tobacco.

Ashley was a banjo picker and, in 1938, toured with the Grand Ole Opry. Playing concerts in such places as New York City, Philadelphia, Washington, DC, and New Brunswick, he wrote frequent postcards home to Myrtie, often more than one each day. On stage he told tales and demonstrated calling cattle, and played "Free a Little Bird," "Married Me a Wife," and his granddad Will's hunting song. Falling asleep in his hotel room after each concert, he said he dreamed he was back home in Walker Valley. On March 1, 1941, while he was checking his traplines in Wear Cove, he suffered a stroke. He built a fire to keep warm and attract attention. He was taken to a nearby house where Myrtie came to see him. She asked him what was wrong. "I don't know, Sweetheart," he told her. "I may live for years, or I may live for months or weeks yet, or I may die tonight." That same night, with Myrtie by his side, he died.

Dora and Lillie Stinnett after three years at Maryville College.

had twelve children together, only one of whom died in infancy. Both Nancy and Mary Ann performed midwife duties for Moll's children.

The living situation must have been difficult for Mary Ann Moore to explain to relatives. Her brother Loon Grant Moore came to rescue her upon hearing the news of his sister taking up with a married man. He liked Will Walker and the pretty green valley so much, however, that he decided to stay. Before long he would become a double relation to Will, marrying Will and Nancy's daughter Betty Ann Walker.

Moll Stinnett brought much of her family with her. Her parents, Ben and Millie, and two of her brothers made Walker Valley their home for many years. One brother, Preacher John Stinnett, would likewise become Will's double relation, marrying his daughter Mary Jane Walker.

Since only Nancy's children could legally bear the Walker name, children born to Mary Ann Moore and Moll Stinnett bore their mother's last name. Over the years both of them became known as Will Walker's "common-law" wives. Tennessee law, however, does not recognize common-law marriages, so the term is incorrectly applied. However, Will cared for them and treated them as his wives no less than he did Nancy. At night he would sing outside his cabin within hearing distance of all three mothers of his children.

It is said that Will took a fourth wife. Little is known about Susan Turner, or Aunt Sukey as she was called by the people of Walker Valley. An African-American and a member of the nearby Meigs Mountain community, she was

Walker Valley school group. You can see some of the Stinnett children in the first row, 1905.

well liked. A former slave, she may have served as a maid to Logan Turner and his wife who moved to the region from North Carolina. According to one account, Sukey bore Logan's children following the death of his wife. George Turner is her only known offspring, and most people believe that Will was the father. Will never claimed him as such, however, saying that if he'd fathered her son he would admit it because he was proud of him and considered him to be a fine young man. Mary Ann is said to have raised him, and when George grew up he fell in love with Birdie Wilson. Fearing prejudice resulting from a mixed-race marriage, George cut his finger and Birdie drank his blood so that she could claim that African-American blood flowed through her veins.

Newspaper articles erroneously described Will and Nancy as Mormons and wildly inflated the number of Will's offspring. While no one knows for certain how many children he had, he produced no more than twenty-seven by Nancy Walker, Mary Ann Moore, and Moll Stinnett. At any given time there were many mouths to feed, but not so many that he couldn't provide for them all.

The task of clothing them all fell to the women. Children went barefoot much of the year, saving their shoes for the winter months. When the time came for a new pair, the child's feet were measured with a stick which was taken to Tuckaleechee Cove so a purchase could be made.

As Will's progeny increased, so did his need for more income. The greatest

Fred Webb: 'Bishop' of Walker Valley

Frederic Webb and his mother Emilie were at first looked upon with distrust but quickly became beloved members of the community during the two summers they lived in Walker Valley. Moll Stinnett even named a child after Emilie. Religion was a driving force behind the education movement during the Progressive Era at the turn of the century, and so Fred was a teacher and a preacher. Though he did not approve of Will's lifestyle (in his journal he lamented the birth of a baby girl to Moll Stinnett, calling the occasion "very discouraging"), he did not judge him publicly. He likewise tolerated many of the superstitions held by some residents. Will Walker, for one, believed that doing business or leaving his cabin was unlucky if a woman came to his home before breakfast.

Fred conducted church services and Sunday school several times each week. Men who attended the meetings enjoyed the singing very much, but they seemed to Fred to have very low expectations for themselves. One Sunday he preached a sermon titled, "Daniel, a Young Man with a Purpose." When that didn't do the trick he preached on "The Last Judgment," writing in his journal afterward, "There were plenty there who should turn their minds toward the end of things. Laid it on stiff as I dared." At the end of each service he asked anyone attending who desired to "do better" to raise their hands. Many usually did, but never all.

Until a proper cottage for Fred and his mother to live in was complete,

L. Harrison Moore, son of Will Walker and Mary Ann Moore, with a bear over his shoulder. Apparently he carried on the family tradition of bear hunting in the Smokies.

source of money came from buying and selling cattle. Business trips took him to such places as Wear Cove, where according to some accounts, he made time for female companionship among other women. Afterward he drove his newly purchased cattle back to his valley to graze them in places where grass grew in forest gaps caused by natural disturbances. He made additional money from farmers outside the area looking for summer pasture, charging a dollar per head of cattle for the season.

Animal pelts provided more income still. With the help of traplines and his rifle "Ol' Death," he sold skins from bears, raccoons, and other wild animals to buyers who carried off their prized goods piled on pack horses. Each spring

Will made sure his homemade steel bear traps were retrieved before a cow stepped in one during the grazing season. He carried the traps, weighing sixty pounds each, home by hand until he was seventy years old.

Illicit whiskey-making was as common in Walker Valley as it was in other mountain hollows. Will himself didn't make it and drank very little. Corn whiskey, though, made for a handy remedy for curing numerous ailments, including snakebite. Whiskey, it was believed, killed the poison, so moonshine was poured into the bite as well as down the throat of the snake-bit person until the victim started vomiting. Mary Ann Moore had a reputation as a "medicine woman" and used moonshine in her homemade cherry cough medicine recipe.

If a death occurred in the community, the funeral was held at home. Neighbors would sit up all night with the deceased. Such occasions were somber and provided little relief other than the moments when the men-folk would slip outside to pass around a fruit jar.

Good Times

Life wasn't all work. During what little time Will Walker spent indoors he might have read the Bible, the Almanac, or the biography of the life of Ulysses S. Grant that he owned. Yarns would

he lived, taught, and preached all in the same room. "Myriads of fleas made it their dwelling-place; hornets and wasps buzzed over our heads all day long, while toads hopped about the floor at night, and numerous rats and mice rattled up and down the old stone chimney," Emilie wrote. Cows and chickens tried entering through the front door which opened onto a pasture. Pet dog Dewey would no sooner drive them back than a curious calf would try to enter once more. Each day the beds were pushed against the walls and possessions moved into the yard and benches carried inside. Emilie took Fred's place teaching morning class while he worked on the cottage alongside Will; then he'd teach in the afternoon and after dismissal work once more on constructing the teacherage. After supper he tutored pupils privately. The days were long and exhausting, but he was doing God's work.

Fred's moral authority as teacher and preacher granted him the honor, or burden, of settling quarrels between residents, such as when Eliza Moore Strickland was cut with a knife by a woman who'd taken up with her son. Few disputes were so gruesome, however, and on one occasion he found himself to be the source of conflict. W.E. Hodge wrote him a letter complaining about the "water closet" Fred had erected in his cornfield.

Fred had a favorite spot on Fodderstack Mountain, and while visiting it in the summer of 1904 he proposed to Clara Liebchen, visiting from Cincinnati, who became his wife.

Moll Stinnett (front, left) and Nancy Caylor Walker with some of Moll's children.

be told around the glow of firelight, including one about the power of some humans to take on the form of animals for the purpose of harming others, much like werewolves in stories originating in Europe.

Good music wasn't hard to find. Ashley Moore was Will's favorite grandson and many evenings Will would stop outside his cabin and holler, "Heeeey Ashley, bring your banjer!" Others would hear it and gather at the Walker place to listen to mountain music made by a fine banjo picker.

Big Will was full of life. Well into his seventies he exhibited a talent for jumping up and clicking his heels together twice before he landed. Occasionally he would receive visitors at his door. Whenever someone asked him if it was true that he had twenty-seven or thirty-six or fifty-two children, depending on the asker, he'd reply, "I haven't counted them lately." If he was asked why

Right: Concerned about his children's education, Will lobbied the Blount County Board of Education for a school, then supplied land, lumber, and skills to build the first school in Walker Valley.

he didn't move to town, he said, "I live in the mountains because I love them. When I was young there wasn't anything about them I didn't want to learn."

Some visitors arrived intending to teach him the error of his ways. Yet, if they quoted Scripture at him he'd quote long verses back to them, reminding them about King Solomon's 700 wives and 300 concubines. That usually shut them up.

Sometimes his old friend Hop would visit. Hop was a Cherokee who is said to have brought his entire family and lived in an old chestnut stump on Fodderstack Mountain when he came. For the most part, however, the valley was unknown to the outside world. Soon all of that would change.

Breaking The Spell of Isolation

Before the turn of the twentieth century, the residents of Walker Valley didn't consider themselves "mountain folks" because so far as they knew everybody lived the way they did. Children probably didn't covet things enjoyed by city children because they may not have been aware that such things even existed.

One thing Will Walker knew they should have, however, was a proper education. The problem was that the nearest school lay seven miles away. So

Ol' Berry Learns to Jay

Will Walker had lots of nieces and nephews. Two nephews one time asked for permission to cut some logs on Rattle Snake Ridge (now Lumber Ridge). The young entrepreneurs called themselves the Fist and Skull Logging Company. They used a mule to start the logs down one of their "skids." When the logs picked up enough speed the boys would yell "Jay!" at which point the mule would step aside and let the logs skid down to the river. But mules, the boys soon found out, can be the most stubborn creatures in the world. One day their mule decided he didn't want to work and would not budge no matter what they tried. Their logs were stranded on the mountainside and now they had no way to get them down. Their Uncle Will had a big red ox named Ol' Berry. When they asked to borrow him, Will said, "You boys know that Ol' Berry is a valuable animal. I was offered $100 for him recently. He's never worked in timber. If anything happens to him, you boys will owe me $100."

With their uncle's admonition ringing in their ears, they led Ol' Berry up the ridge, hitched him to his first load of logs, and started him down the skid. When they yelled "Jay!," Ol' Berry did not understand and kept going down the skid till he was out of sight. The boys followed, worried what they would find when they reached the bottom and whether their company profits, already down, would be enough to replace poor Ol' Berry and appease their Uncle Will. Much to their surprise and relief, however, they merely found Ol' Berry

Will traveled twenty-two miles — a long distance back then — to Maryville to pay a visit to the Blount County school board. Someone more prideful might have refused to ask for help, but nothing would stop Will from lobbying for a school in Walker Valley. One imagines that his imposing stature and striking features might have played a role in the administrative officials taking his request seriously.

Self-taxation had funded public education in Tennessee since 1845. By around 1900, however, funds for a new school in Blount County were too few. Thus Will's request was passed along to the Tennessee Federation of Women's Clubs which had recently created a department to combat illiteracy among mountain residents. Affiliated organizations as far away as Ohio raised the first $50 toward a teacher's salary for the Walker Valley Settlement School. The school opened for a two-month summer term in 1901 and was taught by Andrew Dunn.

A new teacher from Cincinnati arrived the following summer. Frederic Webb and his mother Emilie, who'd fallen in love with the place during a visit, would make Walker Valley their home in the summers of 1902 and 1904. In the interim Fred attended seminary. The urbanite noted in his journal that few sounds were audible except those made by cowbells, children, and the roar of the river. "The sound of neither a steam-whistle or church-bell had ever penetrated these mountains," he wrote. At night it was a very dark place, the only light coming from fireplaces peppering the area. Along with education Fred hoped also to provide a spiritual light for the residents of Walker Valley.

The community experienced a series of "firsts" when the pair of strangers arrived in the summer of 1902. The Webbs arrived on horseback and Emilie's dog Dewey, riding like a circus monkey on her lap, was the first pet that many residents had ever known anyone to own. The doors on the new cottage the Webbs were to live in had locks and keys, another first for the valley. Likewise had few people ever seen a washboard, clothespins, or graniteware cooking utensils. Upon seeing a bright red lampshade for the first time, one little girl asked, "Miss Webb, what kind of bloom is that?"

Will set aside land and furnished lumber for the construction of a cottage, which he and Fred set about building.

straddling the largest log, unharmed. Rejoicing, they lead the ox back up the ridge to finish bringing down their logs. Thereafter, each time Ol' Berry heard the boys yell "Jay!" he stepped aside, having learned his lesson well. Bull Branch, a tributary of the Middle Prong, is named for the event.

An ox snaking out logs.

Will Walker and Ol' Berry, ca. 1915.

21

Walker Valley teacherage, said to be the first in the U.S., ca. 1902.

Small with two rooms, it was the first dwelling in the valley to have two porches, doors with locks, and a floor made of sawed lumber. According to Elizabeth Skaggs Bowman, it was listed by the Department of Education as the first "teacherage" (teachers' residence) in the United States.

On July 3, 1902, Fred cut a young poplar log and hauled it to the school, having in mind an Independence Day surprise for the community. At 4:30 the next morning he climbed out of bed and ran Old Glory up Walker Valley's first flag pole. The whole community marveled at the sight. "My flag took their corks under," he wrote. "It wasn't long until Moze [Mose Moore] and Mr. Walker began to fire their guns."

The first church service Fred was to conduct was scheduled to begin at 9:30 a.m. the next day. So many people arrived at 8:00, however, that meeting began a half hour early. His sermon that Sunday, based on Nehemiah's reconstruction of Jerusalem, conveyed the value of cooperative work.

Sixteen pupils whose ages ranged from three to thirty attended the first day of school the following morning. That evening Fred wrote in his journal, "Some of the children are very bashful but Mama is getting that overcome. We had our hammock up and this they at first shied at but finally enjoyed it to the full. They show their lack of training woefully. We sang the school song and with what results! They all sang in 40 different ways. We'll finally come to it."

By the end of the month enrollment doubled. Each student had a tablet, a pencil and a McGuffy Reader. The smallest children sat in cane-bottom chairs in front; behind them all other pupils sat on hard wooden benches. In her report to the Tennessee Federation of Women's Clubs regarding the progress of her and Fred's students, Emilie wrote, "Perhaps the most noticeable improvement was in reading, for at first, on account of their mountain dialect, we had been obliged to correct them at every other word. Next the punctuation was something to be dreaded, and often I have seen their eyes fill with tears when the task seemed especially difficult, yet both teacher and pupil came out victorious in the end."

At the end of the nine-week term, students were given a book and parents a Bible. Pupils from the school would go on to attend the preparatory department at Maryville College almost continuously until the school, taught during its last years by Kate Duggan, closed in 1924.

Walker Valley church group. If you look closely you can see Nancy and Big Will Walker, Mary Ann Moore, plus some of the Stinnett children.

Emma Moore: Blind But Now I See

Emma Moore was the youngest daughter of Loon Grant Moore and his second wife, Margaret Shields. Life was hard for her family. Her sister Susie drowned in the Middle Prong one cold January day when the foot log was icy. Another sister, Anne, was shot and killed as she was walking down a path with her mother. The killer, her ex-husband Henry Walker, was later declared mentally ill and spent the rest of his life as a cook in an asylum for the insane.

Emma herself was born blind. She begged and cried to go to school like the other children, but the school teacher was not trained to teach blind children. Her uncle Will Walker arranged for her to be sent to a school for the blind in Nashville. It was a long ways from her kin and the valley where she'd been born, but doctors there corrected her vision. She'd never set eyes on her parents before and wasn't sure who to look for after arriving by train back home at the station in Tuckaleechee Cove.

A woman's voice said, "I'm supposed to have a little girl on this train." Recognizing her mother's voice, she ran to her saying, "I'm Emma. I'm your little girl." Before she was convinced that Loon Grant was really her father, though, she felt his face with her hands just like she'd always done.

Some of her fondest memories were riding on the shoulders of Uncle Will and her father who both taught her many things about the trees, flowers, and animals in the forest. Emma Moore described

Splash-Logging

Economics, like education, also contributed to making Walker Valley less remote. Timbering operations by well-financed lumber companies had logged out most of the East and upper Midwest. Soon they would swarm to the blank spot on the map in the heart of the southern Appalachians—the Great Smokies—and forever change their character.

Before then, the practice of logging was a small, local enterprise. The forest held an amazing diversity of tree species. Cutting, while it was hard work, was the easy part; the difficulty came in figuring out how to get the logs to the mill miles away. Splash-logging was the preferred method for accomplishing this, whereby logs were skidded by horses to a temporary dam in the river. When the dam was released, the water carried the logs downstream.

Due to the unpredictable nature of rivers, splash-logging was unsuccessful in many watersheds in the Smokies from a business point of view. Boulders jammed logs, and on sharp bends the river stranded them high on the bank. Yet the practice was more successful in Walker Valley than most places. One observer called the Middle Prong "the best driving stream [for logs] along the northern slope of the Smoky Mountains."

Sometime in the 1890s, Will Walker

struck a deal with the English Lumber Company. The path connecting Walker Valley with Tuckaleechee Cove was rough and narrow. In exchange for English improving it, he granted the splash-loggers access to Spruce Flats Branch. There, at its mouth, they built a dam and floated ash and tuliptree logs, bought from Will for their buoyancy, to the mill in Rockford.

Cutting by the splash dam method was limited to areas easily accessible along streams and rivers, thus causing fewer disturbances to the forest compared with what would soon come. It was a simple operation that relied on little more than sawyers for building a dam, lumberjacks for felling trees, and horses for skidding them to the river. Yet farmers elsewhere in the mountains where the English Lumber Company operated became angry when torrents of water flooded their fields and ruined their crops. Faced with lawsuits and the inability to compete with the Little River Lumber Company, which in 1900 began establishing a large milling operation in Tuckaleechee Cove, the modest enterprise went out of business. Horses and splash dams were replaced by heavy equipment such as steam shovels and loaders, overhead skidders, and locomotives—and miles and miles of railroad.

Colonel W.B. Townsend, owner of Little River Lumber Company, had lots of capital and began buying and logging property neighboring Walker Valley. Will

Nancy Walker as the "best woman God ever made. She was good to everybody. She took care of everybody."

Townsend mill and mill pond. There were three mills built at Townsend—the first two were lost to fires in 1906 and the second in 1916. The last mill was dismantled in 1959.

Loading logs onto a flatcar in Little River gorge, 1906.

Most of the Will Walker family. In the center of the back row with a beard and white shirt is Will Walker. In the second row just below Will and to the right is Nancy Walker. The second person to the right of Nancy is Moll Stinnett, and to the right of Moll is Mary Ann Moore.

In the front row beginning with the second child from the right are six of Moll's children (see pages 15 and 20), including the girl standing behind the bench. The other people in the photo can't be positively identified, but among them are some of Will's grown children and members of Will's extended fam-

Disputes among people in places as remote as Walker Valley were usually settled peacefully, but not always. When tempers flared sometimes someone would take matters into his own hands, and when one such occasion occurred in April 1910, it resulted in tragedy. A good hunting dog was almost as important as a good rifle. Dogs roamed freely in the mountains, often in packs, baying whenever they caught the scent of an animal. Shooting one was unthinkable. A group of settlers in a neighboring valley kept a sheep pen. When dogs belonging to people who lived in Walker Valley broke into it, their predatory instincts took over and they started killing the sheep. The men who owned the sheep tried calling them off, but the dogs, not recognizing the voices as their masters', ignored them. Knowing their entire flock would be lost if they did not act soon, the men began shooting the dogs. The few dogs that survived limped bloodily back to their masters in Walker Valley.

Some individual, or perhaps several, enraged that anyone would shoot his dog, decided to seek revenge and set fire to the woods along the ridge separating the two valleys. The wind, however, changed direction. It was dry that year — so dry that in spring many fields couldn't be plowed — and the fire spread quickly. Among the firefighters was Sam Cook, an expert woodsman who lived in the Spicewoods and for whom a creek, a gap, and a mountain were later named. His son Dock and his daughters Eva and Vannie helped carry water for the men fighting the fire. Vannie was a small,

Walker, though, vowed that he would never sell out to the lumber companies. He liked the mountains just as they were and continued conserving the natural resources under his care. "He never would have let the lumber companies come in here," said Elsie Burrell decades later. He was advised to enter a claim on his land since he possessed no deed. In order to deter officials from judging that he didn't need all his land because no one was living in so many parts of it, he built a possession cabin in each section of the eight square miles he claimed and planted corn.

Dusk Falls

Will fathered his last child when he was well into his seventies. But his and Nancy's last years of life were hard, all the more so while living in such an isolated setting. In the final years, no beef cattle remained. Beehives were left un-robbed, cows un-milked, and hogs un-butchered. They simply didn't have enough energy to perform all the many tasks required for subsisting directly off the land. Too weak even to cut firewood, Will dragged whole fence rails inside the cabin to burn in the fireplace. One visitor reported seeing a fence rail eighteen feet in length sticking out the front door—a testament to how cold the cabin must have remained even with a fire and to how abandoned Will and Nancy must have felt in their old age. According to Arnold Thompson, one of Will's kinfolk who was particularly devout made life hell for Will in his last years, telling him that he was paying for all the sins he'd committed all his life.

A stroke disabled Will in 1918. Colonel Townsend learned of the news and made the trip to the Walker cabin, likely figuring that Will was in desperate need of money to support himself and Nancy, and might at last sell his land. As he lay dying, Will accepted Townsend's offer to purchase 96.25 acres located in one of his favorite haunts along Thunderhead Prong for $1,500, but solely on the condition that it never be cut.

On December 30 of the following year Will suffered another stroke which killed him. The patriarch of Walker Valley was dead.

A mortician from Maryville was called to the cabin to embalm the body. Over the years Will had made coffins for many people who were buried in the cemetery located a stone's throw across the river. It was where Will, too, had long thought he would find his final resting place. But it was not to be. A casket bought in Maryville by several of his children, or perhaps by Colonel Townsend, arrived by train at the Forks of the River

pretty child and liked to make people happy. She was the brightest student in school and was an ace in spelling bees. Dock was asked to help establish a fire line, and the girls were told to sit under a tree and watch the line to make sure the fire didn't jump it. Eva would say later, "It looked like the whole world was burning up." The fire never did jump the line so far as Eva and Vannie could tell, at least not at the ground level. But it did jump from one tree crown to another high in the canopy, which was easily overlooked in daytime amidst all the smoke. Seeing that the crown of the tree under which the girls were sitting had caught fire, Dock hollered, "Look out!" Eva ran one way and Vannie the other. As Vannie was trying to escape, a limb fell and mortally wounded her. Her death traumatized the community and produced a long-standing silence. The story is told that after she was carried to her home in the Spicewoods, a white dove alighted on the windowsill and at the moment of her death disappeared into the ceiling rafters and was never seen again. It came, some said, to guide her home.

Dogs weren't usually pets in the mountains—a good hunting dog was essential for tracking game for the table.

29

and was carried by hand the rest of the way to the cabin. Pairs of men took turns carrying Will's body along the treacherous path leading out of the valley. The river was up that New Year's Eve, and near-freezing temperatures made the task more difficult still.

When the funeral procession reached the mouth of the Middle Prong, a train provided by Colonel Townsend carried Will to the Bethel Baptist Church cemetery. Nancy did not attend the funeral.

Will, according to niece Emma Moore, would not have wanted to be buried in town. "He wanted to be buried up here on the hill where he could look back on all his land where he homesteaded." It would likely have surprised him that the congregation that "churched" him years earlier for his polygamist lifestyle reclaimed him in the end.

Mary Ann Moore died the following year and was buried in the Walker Valley cemetery. A few years later Moll Stinnett and some of her children, attracted by a government land deal, moved to Arkansas. Nancy continued living in the cabin until her own death in 1922, having outlived her husband and all seven of her children. The day she was carried out of the valley in a coffin was the first time she'd left it since the day she arrived sixty-three years before. She'd spent much of her life helping to birth and raise offspring her husband sired through other wives. But laid to rest at last beside Will, she didn't have to share him any longer.

Will had suspected he would die before Nancy and had worried what would become of her after his death. He willed his property to four of his daughters by Moll Stinnett—Dora, Sally, Millie, and Lillie—under the condition that they care for Nancy for the remainder of her life. And so upon her death the land became theirs. They saw no future for themselves in Walker Valley, however. Living in the isolated glen was hard and opportunities for making a better life lay elsewhere. Thus when Colonel Townsend offered to buy their land they agreed to sell it. A new road was cut and rail was laid. Loggers and their families moved in and practically overnight a company town several miles upstream shot up. Close to twenty years passed by as Will's wilderness disappeared acre by acre.

One grove of trees was left to stand. The one along Thunderhead Prong Will had made Colonel Townsend promise not to cut. Will of course had not wished for any part of his valley to be leveled, even after his death. Perhaps, though, he'd suspected that what he'd held near and dear to his heart would not be valued so highly by his children, and he knew that they would sell.

Below is the Stinnett farm; the two figures at left bottom are the same two people in the photo above, Millie and Ben Stinnett. They were Moll Stinnett's parents.

Townsend was a trustworthy man and Will perhaps thought, too, that at least one corner of his wilderness would remain untouched. It's hard to say. At any rate, Colonel Townsend honored his promise for the rest of his life. But in 1936, two years before logging would cease, he himself died.

Upon Colonel Townsend's death, the Walker property was resurveyed and it was discovered that Will had been compensated for only a fraction of the land that had belonged to him. The original survey work had been completed by a man Will hired who'd also been in the employ of the Little River Lumber Company—a conflict of interests that resulted in the company's favor.

But it was too late now. Saws were sharpened and the ancient stand of hemlocks, chestnut and tuliptrees along Will's beloved Thunderhead Prong came crashing to the ground.

END OF THE WILDERNESS

HAD HE LIVED TO 100, WILL WALKER WOULD NOT HAVE RECOGNIZED WHAT became of his valley in the 1920s and 30s. Skidders left indelible marks on the landscape as teams of loggers with crosscut saws scalped the mountainsides. Steam locomotives chugged up and down one hollow after the next hauling lumber to the mill in Tuckaleechee Cove, now called Townsend. Smoke from burning piles of "slash"—the detritus left behind by woodcutters —filled the air for weeks at a time.

People numbering between 1,000 and 2,000 made the valley their temporary home over the course of a decade. The greatest concentration of people resided three miles upstream of the original Walker family settlement at the headwaters of the Middle Prong. Railroad tracks leading to the spot were laid beginning in 1924 and within two years a logging town was born. The valley's first post office opened there on February 13, 1926. A Walker Valley already existed in Tennessee, so Flo Dew and Stuart McNiell, W. B. Townsend's secretary and office manager respectively, chose Tremont. Tree and mountain sandwiched together seemed an obvious choice given the surroundings, though, according to Dwight McCarter, a great-grandson of Mary Ann Moore, the name also aptly describes the three ("tre-") mountains whose feet meet where the town once sat at the forks of the river.

Little evidence remains of the company town today, but in its day it was the thriving epicenter of activity in the valley. A two-story hotel with twenty-two rooms housed company executives and the school teacher, and, later on, tourists. A general store sold staple foods, tools, clothing and livestock feed in exchange for hard cash or, more commonly, company scrip called "doogaloo." The largest building was the machine shop, which serviced and maintained Shay locomotives, railcars, skidders, and loaders.

A multi-purpose building functioned as a schoolhouse during the week,

Life in Stringtown

Life in Stringtown, a logging camp made from portable railroad "car shacks," was full of challenges. One summer rats invaded, running across floors, feeding in pigs' troughs, and eating chicks. For the period of a month people did not venture outside without a broom or garden hoe for protection. In wintertime snow blew into the car shacks, which were full of cracks. In the morning Dorie Cope would wake to find snow on her bedcovers. One time she found her pet gold fish motionless and discovered that the water in the bowl had frozen solid overnight. To revive them she poured warm water over the ice. It cracked and thawed, freeing the fish which began swimming as if nothing had happened. Going to the bathroom could even be dangerous. Polly Watson remembers her mother fearing for her safety whenever she visited the outhouse which sat near a skidder. "Now Pauline," she'd say, "you hurry, because that thing may dump one of those logs right on top of the toilet!" When tragedy visited families in the logging camp, it struck hard. A flu epidemic in 1935 killed thirteen children between the communities in Walker Valley and Elkmont. Yet life in Stringtown was full of joy and humor too. Dorie Cope's family owned a "frustrated" sheepdog. "He was excellent at rounding up the cows and bringing them home. There was one problem — he'd get them mixed up and bring them home in the middle of the day. We herded them back

A portable logging house or "car shack" owned by Little River Lumber Company. These early "mobile homes" could be lifted on and off flat cars.

a sanctuary for worship on Sunday mornings, and a movie theater on Saturday nights, thus earning it the nickname "The House of Education, Salvation, and Damnation." School was held eight months of the year for first through eighth grades. Students wishing to attend high school had to go to Townsend or someplace else. The denominations that worshipped in the building—Methodist, Holiness, Missionary Baptist, Primitive Baptist, Footwashing Baptists, and sometimes Presbyterians and Campbellites— reflected the diverse backgrounds and transient lifestyle lived by people working for the timber industry.

Loggers, rail workers and their families made their homes in four or five camps, each known as Stringtown, that lined the railroad. Each one-room house was 12' x 12', though some renters enlarged their homes by placing two or three together. Precursors to modern mobile homes, they were called "car shacks" or "set off" houses, due to the ease with which they were picked up by a crane and set on a railcar for transport to the next camp. A water-powered generator, or "dynamo," supplied electricity for the machine shop, store, hotel, doctor's office, multipurpose building, and several private residences, but not for Stringtown. There was no insulation whatsoever in the car shacks, and wood heaters provided only a modest amount of comfort. "When your fire went out you just went to bed," said Arnold Thompson.

Woodcutters worked in three-man teams using crosscut saws eleven feet in length for the biggest trees. Rising early and returning home late, men labored ten hours a day, six days a week. Splash-logging was still practiced in places, including one at the mouth of Marks Creek. Since skidding logs behind horses on flume-like rails was difficult in rough mountainous terrain, Little River Lumber

to the open pasture and wondered how we could teach a dog to tell time." The itinerant lifestyle of many lumbering families hardly leant time to get to know any one place very well before it was time to move on. Some people, though, felt deeply connected to their mountain home. For them, bidding farewell to Walker Valley was very hard when the logging boom ended and the national park came. Some men landed jobs with the Aluminum Company of America (ALCOA). Others, like Arnold Thompson, found a job working for the national park. Adapting to suburbia meant adjusting to a very different world. Dorie, for one, found that raising a family in the mountains was far easier than in Knoxville where economic inequality, materialism, and temptations for her children presented unforeseen challenges. Whether they lived in a city or the country, though, they would always be mountain folk.

Colonel W. B. Townsend was the president of Little River Lumber Company. Townsend, the small town that grew up around the lumber mill, was named for him.

"The House of Education, Salvation, and Damnation."

Company encouraged the design of new types of machinery.

Clyde "overhead" skidders used steel cables 3,500 feet in length to drag logs to waiting railcars. Skidder Number Five at Tremont used a cable a mile in length—longer than any other skidder operating in the Smokies. At the end of the line a loader grabbed a log with two giant claws and swung it onto a waiting railcar.

Seven men bearing job titles such as "landing jack" and "jangle ball hooker" were needed to operate each skidder. It was the job of bellboys to communicate to the engineer by hollering signals over a long distance in the woods. "It was an awful damage to the undergrowth timber, skidders were," said Arnold Thompson who eventually worked nearly every position on the skidder team.

The work was dangerous and, at times, fatal. Fifteen-year-old Wesley "Pete" McCarter was put in charge of a jack being used to right an overturned skidder. The jack was under tremendous pressure, and when it slipped, the handle caught him under his chin, instantly breaking his neck. He is buried in the Walker cemetery.

Little River Lumber Company was in many ways ahead of its time in looking after its people. During the same period when coal miners in other parts of Appalachia were suffering inhuman conditions, Little River, for instance, provided health care for workers and their families. At a cost of $1.70 a month per employee, Dr. Bruce Montgomery was available in an office he kept for many years in a two-room car shack. Colonel Townsend was personally known to give college scholarships to his employees' children, and every year his wife brought Christmas gifts for all the families who lived in Stringtown.

A baseball field adjacent to the school provided employees and their children the opportunity to pursue the national pastime. Colonel Townsend's considerable finances allowed him to hire semi-pro ball players to work little during the week and play excellent baseball on the weekends.

Disease, however, found easy purchase in the cramped car shacks, and if the man of the house fell ill or was injured, thus drawing no wages, the entire family became dependent on the good will of neighbors and friends in order to pay the bills. In the early 1930s a worker based at Tremont earned roughly $32 ($400 in today's money) every two weeks. Of this amount, logger Jim Rudd paid $3 to rent a car shack, $1.54 for electricity, $1.10 for insurance, several dollars for ice for refrigeration, and over $20 at the general store. Owing one's soul to the company store, as the song goes, was all too often the case for many individuals. Rudd had only $4.27 left over to feed his family for the next two weeks. Additional groceries along with ice, which wouldn't last that long in midsummer, would need to be purchased—on credit of course.

Just as wholesale timbering and the introduction of the "middle man" were

Tremont Hotel

Will Walker in later years on the right with Loon Grant Moore, Mary Ann's brother, making brooms for the tourists.

new to the valley, so was the division of social classes. Stringtown sat strategically out of sight of the Tremont Hotel, and, like the Wonderland Hotel in nearby Elkmont, lumbermen and their families knew they were not welcome there. Said Dorie Cope, wife of skidder Fred Cope, "The Wonderland was a place to wonder about and view with some envy, as the ladies from Knoxville and other far away cities sat on the front porch in their finery and daintily fanned the gnats and flies away from their perfumed, painted faces." Rich people were seen as different and didn't often associate with lumbermen, and vice versa.

Though poverty seemed always to lurk in the shadows, people who worked for Little River Lumber Company—some of them descendants of those who'd settled the area—experienced a quality of life substantially above the subsistence level for the first time. Yet the cost at which such progress came was great. Improving the economy and standard of living for the region was a triumph, but what it took to accomplish it was a tragedy. Fires scalded important topsoil, and erosion carried away more topsoil still. Gone was the great forest Will Walker had hunted and explored and which had blanketed the mountain slopes for millennia. Gone were the speckled trout, their spawning beds covered in mud, along with habitat for woodland creatures whose numbers had grown scarce. Between 1926 and 1929 alone, ninety million board feet of lumber was logged in Walker Valley. Tremont was a boom town that lasted a mere twelve years, and yet the briefest era in the valley's history was also the most destructive.

The similarities and differences between Will Walker and Colonel Townsend are worth noting. Each man had three wives. Both died at age 81 and prized the Great Smoky Mountains, though each for vastly different reasons.

Will Walker managed his land so that it would sustain him and everybody under his watchful care for as long as he lived. For Colonel Townsend, who looked after an even greater number of people, the land was a means for financial gain and economic betterment, yet in an unsustainable way.

When the idea of a national park in the Smokies was born, Colonel Townsend was the first to sell his land—save for the timbering rights—to the Tennessee Park Commission. In December 1938, over four years after the establishment of Great Smoky Mountains National Park, the last trees logged on park land were hauled by train out of Walker Valley. It was the end of another era and the beginning of something new.

Frank and Grant Moore.

DAWN OF A NEW DAY

THE CREATION OF GREAT SMOKY MOUNTAINS NATIONAL PARK PROMISED THE return of the great forest someday, and the renewal of the wilderness Will Walker had fallen in love with decades before. In the meantime, seeds that would bear fruit in Walker Valley for years to come were actually planted long before logging came to an end.

One was a Girl Scout Camp, which opened in 1925. Mable Ijams, Colonel Townsend's daughter, was a member of the Knoxville Girl Scout Council and asked her father to set aside some land held by the Little River Lumber Company for a summer camp. She rode the logging train along the Little River to Elkmont looking for a proper site but found none to her liking. Hiking a mountain at the lower end of Walker Valley, she came to Will and Nancy's old homestead and fell in love with the place.

Camp Margaret Townsend was named in honor of Townsend's wife who had recently died. The lumber company constructed a mess hall, infirmary, latrines and tent platforms on a dozen-acre campus and erected a dam in a side channel of the river where the girls swam, bathed, and did their laundry. Other buildings, including a hut for counselors, were added later. Reflecting the frontier history engrained in the national character, kept alive through camping which was becoming increasingly popular, girls were grouped by age as Hunters, Settlers, Indians, Pioneers, and Gypsies. On overnight trips, girls packed a bedroll and pup tent and learned how to build and cook over a fire. A group of older girls lived separately learning wood crafts, making their own tools, and cooking all their food outdoors.

"Camping promotes wonderful relationships," said Margaret Matthews, who started as drama counselor and eventually became director. Daily activities largely focused on nature. Sherman Stinnett, Will Walker's grandson, worked tirelessly as the camp's caretaker for many years, though the annual job of stuffing mattresses was fulfilled by the board of trustees. Before the camp's

Trail construction on Miry Ridge, 1934-1935.

charter expired, a new camp on a larger tract of land on Norris Lake was created by the Tanasi Girl Scout Council and opened in 1960. Many camp activities begun by the Girl Scouts continue to this day at Great Smoky Mountains Institute at Tremont.

Another seed that would bear fruit in Walker Valley was the establishment of a Civilian Conservation Corps (CCC) camp. The Great Depression put about a quarter of the nation out of work, fostering despondency among many young people over their future. Poverty exploded across the country. Family, community, and religious organizations alone seemed incapable of solving the crisis, so government was looked to as the driving force to lift Americans out of economic despair. The CCC was born out of President Franklin D. Roosevelt's New Deal.

Young men who signed up with the CCC made Walker Valley their home starting in 1933. Company 1461 occupied Camp Willis P. Davis which resided three miles upstream from Tremont logging town and housed 172 men. In 1936, a special board of district officers appraised it as the most outstanding in Tennessee. In five years alone the company constructed thirty-two miles of hiking trails and thirty-five miles of horse trails. They built bridges, fought fires, and maintained a fire lookout tower on Blanket Mountain. Classes in a range of subjects provided additional vocational training for the young men. During off hours they attended dances, stunt nights, pool tournaments, and baseball games. Arts and crafts and a swimming pool offered further opportunities for recreation.

Of the $30 ($460 in today's money) each man earned per month, all but $5 was sent home to his family. Dorie Cope surmised that the food must have been awful. When a young man from the camp who was soon to become her son-in-law came for dinner, he looked with longing at the biscuits and cornbread on the table but was too well-mannered to eat all he wanted. But the CCC boys learned a thing about the woods too, supplementing their diet by catching speckled trout, which they pan-fried with freshly gathered ramps.

Congress abolished the CCC in 1942 at the start of World War II. The notion of investing in young people was resurrected in 1964, however, when a Job Corps Center was established in Walker Valley. By then a small primitive campground resided on the site of Will and Nancy's old homestead, going by the name Tremont, which the park borrowed from the old logging town further up the road. In some ways the Tremont Job Corps was an updated version of the Civilian Conservation Corps. Young men and women maintained trails, cleaned streams, and received training in road-building, masonry and operating heavy machinery. It closed in 1969 after the government decided it was too small an operation to justify the expense.

That same year, Elsie Burrell, along with a cadre of school teachers and Maryville College officials, petitioned the National Park Service to turn the abandoned Tremont Job Corps facility into an environmental education center. Following a decade of operation under the auspices of the college, the center was administered for two decades by Great Smoky Mountains Natural History Association (now called Great Smoky Mountains Association), until it eventually became its own independent park partner organization.

CCC work camp (Spike camp) with mess tent in center, ca. 1935.

Girl Scout Rock

Girl Scout Island was a favorite spot among scouts attending Camp Margaret Townsend. Sunday school was often held there. One rock sitting at the head of the island they fancied more than any other. Big and flat, it provided an ideal place for one to close one's eyes and bask in the sun while the river rushed by only a few feet away, carrying off every anxiety. One morning the scouts discovered that three holes had been drilled into their rock. What it meant was no mystery. The lumber company planned to dynamite it so that one less obstacle blocked the logs it wanted to float downstream to the mill in Townsend. Another version of the story says that a road construction crew wanted to use crushed rock pieces as part of a roadbed. The scouts held a meeting and decided to save their rock. A schedule was drawn up and scouts and scout mothers took turns picnicking on the rock every hour of the day. The following morning the men whose job was to blow up the rock showed up, but there were the girl scouts sitting on their rock. The next day the men arrived even earlier only to find the rock occupied once more by a gaggle of girls unwilling to sacrifice a favorite spot for the sake of "progress." After the third day the crew finally gave up. The girl scouts had fought to preserve their rock and won. But the story doesn't end there. Over sixty years later, in 1994, a flood roared down the valley pushing aside boulders and washing away huge sections of the

Today over 5,000 people a year make their home, at least temporarily, in Walker Valley. Groups of all ages visit Great Smoky Mountains Institute at Tremont to live and learn, using the national park as an outdoor classroom. Children and adults experience firsthand the incredible biodiversity of the park by searching for salamanders, or by exploring the Smokies' rich cultural and natural history on wilderness hikes. A sense of belonging and comfort among nature is felt by many for the first time here, as everyone at day's end gathers around a campfire to tell stories and sing songs. Tremont's continued existence helps to preserve and celebrate the lives of the people who have called Walker Valley home.

People & Place

Descendants of Will Walker return to the valley and cemetery once a year for Decoration Day, the first Sunday in June. They keep a good sense of humor about their forebear's exploits with women. "We've reduced the number of children —and number of spouses—with each generation," says Phyllis Stinnett Atchley, one of Will Walker's granddaughters. Will would be proud of the successes of his progeny. Many own their own businesses and a few have become millionaires. More importantly, they've held on to many of the same values of their ancestors. While today people often measure happiness by the accumulation of big houses and big cars and adopting the latest fashions, thanks to stories passed down from one generation to the next, many descendants remember that true happiness means family and working hard for simple necessities. Says Will's great grand-daughter Debbie Rolen Wilbourn, "We have a lot of faith and hope, and a lot of love. No pun intended."

Will Walker likewise would have been proud of Great Smoky Mountains Institute at Tremont, said Wilma Dykeman. "The story of Tremont

road. Many people called it a "century flood" because one that size is said to occur only every hundred years, (though another one almost as big happened again in 2003). On both occasions, Girl Scout Rock acted like the bow of a ship, diverting floodwaters around either side of the island. Without it, it's certain that important topsoil would have been washed away leaving no place on the island for trees and plants to grow, birds to find nests, and people to enjoy them. The Girl Scouts didn't know it at the time, but by saving just one rock they were really saving the entire island.

Children enjoying an afternoon outing at Tremont.

culminates the history of the Great Smoky Mountains," she wrote. "For here is one of the ways the Smokies can be best used: as a wild refuge and a living laboratory where young people may discover the deeper meaning of the park's past and why, for the future, there is a park at all."

The story of Walker Valley is one of people and place. Of gaining a sense of place, and of people learning to take care of their place on earth along with all the earth's resources. It's a story that isn't over, and if you haven't already, perhaps someday you'll find yourself a part of it too.

School group learning about aquatic life at Tremont.

Elsie Burrell and others in historical costume at Little Greenbrier School. Elsie was renowned for her interpretations of early life in the Smokies and support for Great Smoky Mountains Institute at Tremont.

46

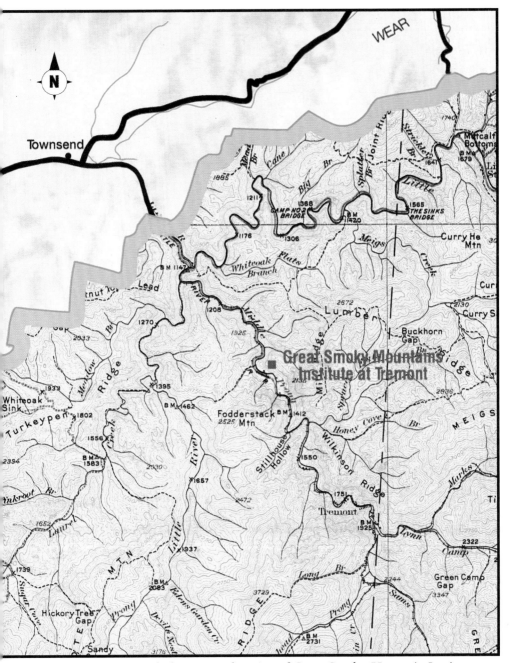

1930s U.S.G.S map with the current location of Great Smoky Mountain Institute at Tremont added.

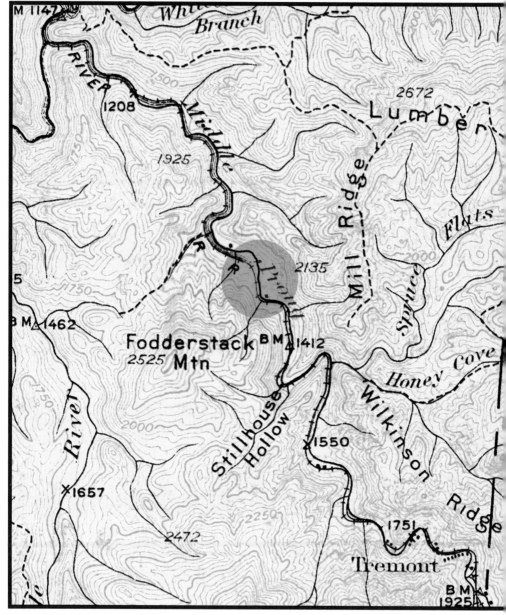

This enlargement of the 1930s map shows the location of Walker Valley in green.

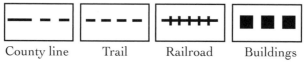

| County line | Trail | Railroad | Buildings |

I've found a home in Walker Valley,

I'll return though I travel far away,

Tremont holds a piece of my soul,

Great Smoky Mountains, I'll be back some other day.

From the song "A Home in Walker Valley"
—by Ken Voorhis

Acknowledgments:

The author wishes to express the debt he owes to two individuals without whom this book could not have been written: Elsie Burrell, who collected many stories about Walker Valley during her lifetime, and Lloyd Foster, who produced numerous invaluable interviews with people who once resided in the valley.

Thanks to the following people for the assistance they provided in a number of ways: Ken Voorhis, Robin Goddard, Pat Dorsey, Dwight McCarter, Connie Millar, Julie Brown, Amber Parker, Tom Taylor and Annette Hartigan. Thanks also to Steve Kemp.

Finally, a special thanks to the Hambidge Center for Creative Arts and Sciences for providing a quiet space to write.

Author Jeremy Lloyd teaches at Great Smoky Mountains Institute at Tremont and is the author of *Great Smoky Mountains National Park Pocket Guide & Journal.* He is a frequent contributor to *Smokies Life* magazine and the *Bearpaw* and *Walker Valley Reflections* newsletters.

Published in the United States by Great Smoky Mountains Association.
Great Smoky Mountains Association is a private, nonprofit organization which supports the educational, scientific, and historical programs of Great Smoky Mountains National Park. Our publications are an educational service intended to enhance the public's understanding and enjoyment of the national park. If you would like to know more about our publications, memberships, guided hikes and other projects, please contact:
Great Smoky Mountains Association
115 Park Headquarters Rd.
Gatlinburg, TN 37738
(865) 436-7318
www.SmokiesInformation.org

ISBN: 978-0-937207-62-8

Editors: Steve Kemp and Kent Cave
Illustration and book design: Joey Heath
Editorial assistance: Julie Brown and Valerie Polk
Printed and bound by Chocklett Press, Roanoke, VA.

02 03 04 05 06 07 08 09